Would you put your money in a sand bank?

TO MY SON STUART

in lively remembrance of
all those many games with words

Would you put your money in a sand bank?

(Fun with Words)

by Harold Longman

illustrated by Abner Graboff

 RAND McNALLY & COMPANY

Copyright © 1968 by Harold S. Longman
Copyright 1968 under International Copyright Union
by Harold S. Longman. All rights reserved
Printed in U.S.A.
Third printing, 1971
Library of Congress Catalog Card Number: 68-11649

Fun with Words

We use words in a thousand ways, and for a thousand things.

We use words to describe how a jet plane works, or how to put together a toy rocket. We use words to tell about our dreams, our feelings, our ideas. We write words, read them, sing them, talk them.

We can play with words, too. When we do, we use words to make riddles, rhymes, puns, and jokes—and that's where the fun comes in.

For example, here's a silly question that's a pun:

Would you put your money in a *sand bank?*

Of course not!

Why not?

For the same reason you wouldn't put your money in a *bank of clouds,* or a *riverbank*, or a *snowbank*, or a *bank of oars*, or the bonnie *banks of Loch Lomond.*

Those are not the kinds of banks where money is kept, of course. You know that so well that you don't even think about it. That's why it's a silly question. It's also a pun because it's a play on words—using one word in place of another, when both words sound the same, but mean different things.

Why is it that we use the same words to mean so many different things? Because they're not really the same words at all—even though they happen to sound the same or look the same.

Words that sound like other words, but are spelled differently—*peak* and *peek*, for example—are called homonyms. Words that sound the same and are also spelled the same—*bank* and *bank*, for example—are usually called homonyms, too, and sometimes homophones.

How does it happen that they sound alike, or look alike, or both?

Because that's how it happened, a long time ago.

Words have a history, just like people. And when times change, words change with them.

Take *peak*. It comes from the Old English word *peac*, which meant a hilly place. Old English was spoken in the sixth century, in the days of the Angles and Saxons, in ancient Britain.

Peek came from the Middle English word *pike*, about 600 years later. Old English had changed to Middle English by then, and a great change it was. The Saxons had been conquered by William of Normandy, and with him, many French words came into the language. *Pike* meant to look through a crevice, and in French would be pronounced "peek." Because it was pronounced that way, people came to spell it that way. And because *peak* and *peek* sound alike, you can make a pun and a riddle with them:

Why was the mountain top flat when the mountain climber came back?

Because he took a *peek* from the top.

In the answer, you're using one sound-alike homonym in place of another, so it's a pun. Because the question is meant to puzzle you, and because it has an unexpected answer, it's a riddle.

The word *bank* has a different history. One meaning comes from the Old Norse, the language that Leif Ericson spoke when he sailed in his Viking ship. It meant (and still does) a raised shelf, or ridge of ground.

A different word, with a different meaning, but now spelled exactly the same way, came from the Latin. It meant (and still does) a seat, especially in a store. From a seat in a store, it came to mean a counter in a store. From that, it came to mean the counter in a money-changer's shop, and from there it was an easy step to the kind of bank where money is kept. And the word is still taking on new meanings! Today, we have blood banks, atomic banks, memory banks, and lots of other kinds of banks the Romans never dreamed of. So *bank* is coming to mean any place where anything is stored. Quite a difference from a seat in a store!

There are lots of homonyms in our language, and in all languages. Have fun with them!

By the way—can you carve your initials in the *bark* of a dog?

Riddles, Riddles, Riddles

1. Why should you build your house in a ball field?
   Because every house needs a *base*.

2. Why is a game of baseball like a pancake?
   Because they both need *batters*.

3. Why was Cinderella thrown off the baseball team?
   Because she ran away from the *ball*.

4. What kind of beams are never used for building, but are found in every house?
   Beams of light.

5. Why did the groceryman sue the pelican?
   Because the pelican had too big a *bill*.

6. Why couldn't King Arthur find his *page?*
   He had closed his book.

7. What's the best place to hide a lawyer?
   In a legal *case.*

8. What kind of log floats without touching water?
   A ship's *log.*

9. Why does a *pine* tree *pine?*
   Because it can never grow an ice-cream *cone.*

10. What's the most social kind of tree there is?
    A *date* tree.

11. Why should you go to an ironworks to find something you've lost?
    Because it's a *foundry.*

12. If animals played baseball, which one would hit hardest?
    A *bat.*

13. When is a boy not a boy?
    When he's a little *hoarse.*

14. What's the spiciest animal known?
    A *curried* horse.

15. When is the tail of a horse like a ship?
    When it's *docked*.

16. Why did King Solomon send a wastepaper basket to the Queen of Sheba?
    He heard that she always traveled in a *litter*.

17. Which is the hardest time of the year for a soldier in the army?
    The thirty-one days of *March!*

18. Why did the pirates paint the prisoner's face dark red when they left him on a desert island?
    They wanted to *maroon* him.

19. Why did the zookeeper run after the lady?
    Because she had a *mole* on her nose.

Silly Questions

Can you think of one answer that will fit all of these questions? Careful now—it's tricky!

1. If corn can't hear, why does it have an *ear*?
2. Why can't you hit anything with a ball *club*?
3. Why do you *long* for a vacation if a vacation is never *long* enough?
4. What's so *fine* about a *fine*?
5. How long does the human *race* take?

6. Do *beetle* brows make you look bug-eyed?

7. Can a sea horse swim farther than a *bay* horse?

8. If you were trying to put up a *fence* faster than your neighbor, would you call it a *fencing* match?

9. If you spent lots of time combing your long hair, would you call it your *mane* interest?

10. Can you fasten a door with a *lock* of hair?

11. Would you call a fisherman's catch his *net* results?

12. When two horses go up the *bridle* path together, does that mean they're getting married?

13. If you got lost in the fog, would you say you had *mist* your way?

14. If a bird fell into a chimney, would you say it *flue* down?

15. When cotton is put on the scales down south, would you say they *weigh* down upon the Swanee River?

16. If a king *reigns* over a kingdom, would the kingdom be wet all the time?

17. If a landlady heard a tenant talking in the next room, would she be hearing a *rumor?*
18. Would a man who runs a bargain basement be called a *seller* in a *cellar?*
19. When a doctor says, "You must learn to relax," does he mean you have to be *taught* not to be *taut?*

20. Would you call a short sleep a *napkin?*
21. When everyone says, "It's a lovely day," does that make the weather *vain?*
22. If a rescue party took all day to save some people lost in the snow, would you call that an all-day *succor?*
23. When you put *rings* on your fingers, do you *wring* your hands?
24. Can you *write* a wrong?

Answer: *There's* NO *answer—because there's never a real answer to a silly question!*

Questions with Answers

1. What did the horse say to the stable boy?
   Just give me a little *bit*.

2. What did the piece of wood say to the electric drill?
   You *bore* me.

3. What did the punching bag say to the package-wrapper at the sporting-goods store?
   Box me.

4. What did the fish say when he was caught on the hook?
   Gosh! I thought I knew all the *angles!*

5. Why was the pony called a hot-head?
   Because he had a *blaze* on his forehead.

6. What did the first alligator say to the second alligator?
   Nothing. He had a *frog* in his throat.

7. What did the empty balloon say to the boxer?
    Give me a strong *blow*.

8. What did the piglet say to the man at the stationery store?
    I need a pig *pen*.

9. What did Orpheus say to his harp when its tone wasn't true?
    I'm afraid you're just a *lyre*.

10. What did the property owner say to the trespasser?
    Leave my *site* at once!

11. What did the window say when the baseball hit it?
    I feel fine—my *pane* is gone.

12. What did the Indians say when their rain god didn't send rain?
    That their *idol* was *idle*.

13. What did the wolf say to the sheepskin?
    Hide me.

14. What did the kindling wood say to the fireplace?
    Goodbye! I've met my *match*.

15. What did the prisoners say when the jail was flooded?
    Somebody ought to *bail* us out.

16. What did the fat man say when he sat down to dinner?
    I'm afraid this food is going to *waist*.

17. What did Noah's animals say when they saw the rainbow?
    Look! Another *arc!*

18. What did the ship's captain say to the passengers when the sailors ran away?
    Sorry! No *crews* today.

19. What did the boy say when he decided to sell his bicycle?
    I think I'll *peddle* my bike.

20. What did the steak say to the plate?
    Pleased to *meat* you.

21. What did the bell say to the orange?
    It's strange, but I can't hear your *peel*.

22. What did the cow say to the pig?
    I'm afraid you're just a *boar*.

23. What did the first shipwrecked sailor say when the second sailor was washed ashore?

Now we have two on the *isle*.

24. What did the raisin say to the coffee cake?

I feel like I'm rolling in *dough*.

25. What did the ball say to the tennis player?

Stop! I'm nervous! I can't stand the *racquet!*

26. What did the fly say to his mother when he landed on the man's foot?

Look, Ma—I'm a *shoe fly*.

Some More Riddles

1. When is a shellfish stronger than a shark?
   When it's all *mussel*.

2. Why does an artist lie down when he paints?
   Because he works from his *pallet*.

3. How did the wood shaving fly from the board?
   It took off on a *plane*.

4. Why was the florist suspicious of the flowers?
   He discovered them in a garden *plot*.

5. What species of animal worries most about its weight?
   Fish. They carry their *scales* wherever they go.

6. Which has more to tell—a tall building or a short building?
   A tall building. It has more *stories.*

7. What did the robbers call their orchestra?
   A *steel* band.

8. Why did the soldier have holes in his uniform?
He had been *drilled* all day.

9. Why were the sculptor's hands so cold?
He was carving a *frieze*.

10. Why does a shoemaker work backward?
He starts with his *last* first.

11. Why are squirrels such gossips?
Because they can't help carrying *tails*.

12. Why does the day of a funeral have no afternoon?
Because it's a day of *mourning*.

Nonsense Conversations

Eh? What's That?

"*Phew!*"
"You have only a *few?*"
"No—I'm *through.*"
"You *threw* something?"
"No—I just set a *stake* near the *creek.*"
"It must have been too tough to eat. I never heard a *steak creak* before."

Something New

"What's a *gnu*?"

"You mean, what's *new*?"

"*No*, I *know* what I mean. A *gnu* is some kind of animal."

"Oh—I see. You didn't mean, 'what's *new*,' you meant, 'what's a *gnu*.'"

"That's right. What's a *gnu*?"

"If I *knew*, I'd tell you, but *gnus* are *news* to me."

Conversation with Mother

"May I please have a *pear?*"
"Yes, dear, but *pare* the skin off."
"May I have another?"
"Why didn't you ask for a *pair* in the first place?"

Problem

"Toss me a piece of *stationery*, Joe. I want to write a letter."
"How can I toss it if it's *stationary*?"

Good Knight!

"It says here that every *night*, the *knight* wore a suit of *mail*."

"Maybe he was going to the post office."

"Not the kind of *mail* you *mail*, silly—the kind of *mail* you wear. It's called *chain mail*."

"I got a *chain* letter once, but I didn't wear it."

"*Chain mail* isn't *mail*—I mean, you can wear *chain mail*, but you can't wear a *chain* letter."

"How about a postcard?"

On the Boat

"Watch out! I'm going to lower the *boom!*"
"I don't *hear* any *boom.*"
"The *boom* is right *here,* and *here* it goes!"
"OW!"
"Did you *hear* it that time?"
"Did I *hear* it! My ears are still ringing!"

Goodbye Now!

"Isn't that just *great!*"
"Something wrong with the *grate?*"
"No—something terrible. I just invited the wrong *guest.*"
"You *guessed* wrong?"
"Oh, leave me *alone!*"
"You want a *loan?*"

The Winner

"Which *one won?*"
"Number *two.*"
"*Too* bad. I chose Number *one.*"
"Well, Number *two* is Number *one* since he *won.*"

Just Plain Silly

"The sign says, "*PLANES FOR HIRE.*"
"Does that mean they fly *higher?*"
"Higher than the *plains*, I suppose."
"I should hope so! But suppose you were in the mountains?"
"Well, if you were *over* the mountains, it would be all right,
  but if the mountains were *over* you, it would be all *over*."
"That seems *plain* enough."

Silly Poems

I can *sew* a seam
And I can *sow* a seed.
So—
Wouldn't you know?
People call me a *sew* and *sow*.

I spent a *cent*
To buy some *scent*
And *sent* it to a friend, who wrote:
"This *vial* of stuff
Is *vile* enough
To use for making creosote."

I think that English is sickly.
Words change their meanings so quickly.
"Time goes *fast*," simply means that time's fleeting.
When you *fast*, it just means you're not eating.
And "stuck *fast*" means you're glued to the spot.
So if you go *fast*, you will never be *last*,
If you *fast*, you may *last*, or may not.

A *bear* runs around in a *bear* skin
To keep himself warm when it's freezing.
If you run around in a *bare* skin
You soon will be coughing and wheezing.

A *cock* is a rooster, a robin, a bird,
And as everyone knows, has no eyebrows.
But people, who have them, can easily *cock* them
Whether they're lowbrows or highbrows.

A *haycock*, of course, has nothing to *cock*,
It's just straw in a field standing steady.
And *cocking* a gun is quite different again—
It means you can fire when ready.

If you think this seems strange, or you think it unfair,
Just think of the *cock* with a comb and no hair.

I stood on the *pier* to *peer* at the lake.
A sign on a boat said, "For *Sale*."
So I went for a *sail* and landed in jail—
Could it be that I made a mistake?

A *sole* is a fish one can eat.
And *soles* are the *soles* of your feet.
A *soul,* we are told, is a spirit.
We can't see it or touch it or hear it.

This would all be most amusing
If it weren't so confusing.

If you *raise* a building, it goes up straight and tall.
If you *raze* a building, no building's left at all.
Change a word a little bit
And end up with the opposite.

She was *wrapped* up in a story—
The story held her *rapt*.
She *read* until her eyes were *red*
Was she *wrapped*, or *rapt*, or trapped?

A wicked King named Max
Decreed an income *tax*.
He put a notice on the wall,
And stuck it up with *tacks*.

The people cried, "We can't abide
Either Max or *tax!*
The outcome is, our income
Won't even buy us snacks!

"A plague on Max's *taxes!*
They're anything but fair!
He *taxes* both our income
And our patience, we declare!"

So up they rose upon their toes
And seized all Max's *tacks*. . .
Went marching to the palace
And stuck the *tacks* in Max.

When the prisoner sang a sad ditty,
His jailer was *fired* with deep pity.
"What a shame, what a bore
Not to open his door!
But I'd promptly be *fired* by the city!"

Achilles stood upon his *feet*
Performing *feats* of valor,
When suddenly an arrow struck—
All saw his dreadful pallor.
"My *heel!*" he cried, "it will not *heal!*
I'm through—I'm finished—beat!"
You might say of Achilles
Defeat was in his *feet*.

Let's take the word *"jar."* It means, "make a noise"—
Unpleasant, discordant, or scary.
And a *jar* is a jug for cookies, or jam
Made from some kind of fruit or some berry.

A door left *ajar* is a door that's not closed.
But *a jar* by a door is a danger.
To *jar* someone means to push, or upset—
Not polite to a friend or a stranger.

The language is full of such odd little quirks—
A nuisance, so many folks say.
What nonsense! They're fun! Make a joke or a pun!
Let the homonyms fall where they may!

Printed in U.S.A.